www.finishinglinepress.com

True if Destroyed

poems by

Jamie Gage

Finishing Line Press
Georgetown, Kentucky

True if Destroyed

ACKNOWLEDGMENTS

I'd like to thank the following publications for first publishing these poems:

Green Mountain Trading Post (2004): "Stannard Mountain"
Iconoclast (2004): "Safe Passage"
Inkwell (2006): "Stalker"
Main Street Rag (2006): "Kirkuk"
Mountain Gazette (2007): "Hermit Thrush"
New Verse News (2011): "Memorial Day"
Northern New England Review (2004): "Mollusk"
Out of Line (2006): "Strange Fruit" and "April Snow"
Powhatan Review (2004-2005): "Abundance" and "Pledge"

Editor: Christen Kincaid

Cover Art: Jamie Gage and Fred Van Geloven

Author Photo: Jamie Gage

Cover Design: Elizabeth Maines

Printed in the USA on acid-free paper.
Order online: www.finishinglinepress.com
         also available on amazon.com

Author inquiries and mail orders:
Finishing Line Press
P. O. Box 1626
Georgetown, Kentucky 40324
U. S. A.

Table of Contents

"We can bring our human, distracted love into focus with an act that doesn't need words, an act which dramatizes for us what we are together. The act itself can be anything: five beaten and scrambled eggs, two glasses of wine, running beside each other in rhythm with the pace and breath of the beloved."

—Andre Dubus, "On Charon's Wharf"

Hearts

Abundance

There is something that happens
when we lie down with each other
that is beyond even my
best recollection of ourselves,
beyond this rush of salt air through
the truck's open window or the
unseasonal haze
settled over the bay. It's

October, and you're as clear
in my mind as you've ever been,
as beautiful as words
that I don't need to say
because you are near and because
I have gazed
for so long
through the shade
of your orbit. The fact is,
I have no words for this love:
it is an entity unto itself,
like the clang-call of an ocean buoy,
or your ink-stained, unwavering eyes.

Letters

I have seen your initials
etched carefully
onto a white oak
along the road to your house.
All the innocence
and candor of youth
(hearts-and-arrows, true-if-destroyed)—
cut canyons
in the musky thick bark.

When you were ten they taught you
that if you fell a tree
and count its rings
you would know how long it lived,
and when it died.

A dozen summers since
my old jackknife lies
inside an elementary desk drawer,
its blades now rusted shut:
champion of my childhood,
my own initials a scrawl upon it.

Heroes

It is raining on the seesaw
when he tells me his heroes
Garcia and Mantle are gone.

Six, I want to run
to the jungle jim but
rise up to the rain instead:

there, high above
fulcrum, my father,
and the rage of my tears

I can see a treehouse
through turning maples
and know then he will miss me.

Falling, my knuckles wrap white
to the wet metal bar like Christmas
paper to a whiffle bat or a plastic guitar

as my mother at home packs
pictures with guilt in our rush to
Sun City to mete out memories of you.

Stalker

I can see the window
behind which you wash dishes,
scrubbing the days clean plate after plate,
scanning your hands for any betrayal of age—
a mordant self-portrait on the edge of the forest:
queen of Palmolive, absolution at the sink.

It's long past midnight, and this stand of white pines
behind your wood cabin confers like bishops
in a court full of thieves, laughing interminably.
What else? The sky black as blight
below a smudge of dim stars.

But listen now
as the boughs from a solitary spruce
begin to burst all at once, pouring last night's rain
over the eaves of your roof, over the
squelched metal gutters and your uneven porch—
the screen door rasps, the floorboards moulder,
the hook pulls back on the eyelet.

I said stop crying.

Castrato

I chewed slowly that night
beneath coconut palms
among the South Beach elite,
transfixed by longing
and the specter of passion.

My T-bone was pink—rare—
and my pinot noir had me loose in the ribs.
Louie Prima singing Buono Sera
through the fern-hidden speakers
as my mind moved to a once-known place.
Except for the lust I might call it peace.

Because when the muses arrived
with their Icelandic eyes
and butterscotch legs
I abandoned my post
and threw up my plate.
It was simply too much.

Later among the eunuchs
I would share my blurred vision,
my uncontrolled state. They laughed,
then pitched me in the fire.

Mollusk

Outside my bay window the rains
have stopped, but they'll soon start again.
The beat of heat lightning flickers
from the glass. Your face—

fractured, blissful, astounding,
lost in my own doleful reflection—out to sea
as they say, a hole where once there was sun.

Still these casts of flat beauty
beyond even the taciturn of doubt: a door,
yes, but a door among walls.
Beyond these walls, these nail-bitten doors,
beyond even words and
their careless intransigence I waited. I called.
Where were you.

In the white light the shadows from the trees
draw caricatures that lengthen toward the sea.
But your face doesn't placate the waves, your
voice doesn't drown out the wind.
I gaze out past the red tides
where a sole mollusk gasps,
draws a long breath of air, and waits.

Owl

Lost in the swamp behind Wal-Mart
with nothing but cattails under
the bracken gray light
thrown from the lot,
the LED poles strung up
across this once-rural plain.

But it's different here, clear,
unbroken beneath stars
and quiet, and though
Ginger is gone, or may be gone—
a week now since our yellow lab
bolted from the yard after
a squirrel or a finch
and never came back—
I know that she's safe,
safely harbored somewhere.
I want to believe that.

So I call back the night
and the two nights before it,
my wife keening in the bathroom
when the kids went to sleep.
And the owl, that snow-white owl
who sat stoically atop our chain-link fence
like a sentinel to our friend of ten years
before lighting out
to the cobalt sky of the north:
an apparition at dawn,
the cold cells of my senses.

Origins

From the burped belly of the crater I emerged,
soaked, lava-fed, scourged out onto land.

On the ripped beachhead
clams and obsidian shells glistened
in the mud, luminous shards
blinding and stark.
As the sun spread its last rays
above the blue screed of sea

I felt the old pull, the old primordial urge.
I watched the night move the stars from their orbits.
The tide lapped at my feet like a geisha.

*

In the morning I wake to hear voices,
the bed empty again. No waves framing
the sun, just the hushed flat murmur
of geishas who mock me
from beyond the oak door.

Out the bay window I watch
as my neighbor's college-bound niece
so tan and perfectly firm
leans into her car for something unseen.
Maybe lipstick or a Blow Pop,
a half pack of Camels.

Two hours later I sit rapt
at the glass, eyes trained
on the pavement for her
imminent return.

Children of the Woods

When she hands me an oak leaf
or a fistful of needles for the
fourth time this morning,
I am struck by how much
my daughter resembles her brother,
his summer-brown skin
and half-curled grin, the other half
level with earnestness.

As we round a bend in the root-strewn trail
that we began clearing last weekend,
I can hear Aidan's seesaw cadence
call out from behind a thicket of spruce.
He is singing one of his favorites—
"Old MacDonald"—and when he comes to
the line that he has made up
about his Pigdog friend
with the upturned snout,
I can hear him howling and grunt-barking,
then his sister laughing
through the cone-bearing boughs.

This is the morning I've dreamed of,
that I have forever wanted to live.
These children of the woods
are trees of their own,
above all else I have known.

Stannard Mountain

Caledonia fades
on these nights of no closure,
a foray through the pines
among runaway ghosts.

Always the ghosts
who tempt us to grieve
and not celebrate the silence
of a forest's last snow.

It lights like a cadence
from the woods to your eyes—
that gentle smile,
this wept benediction.

Arrows

My father last night

My father last night
stoked the wood fire
drank the cold draught
ate the T-bone
ignored the doc's calls
cursed the ex-prez
read the good book
gazed at the sky
limped up the stairs
popped all the pills
cranked up the brass
oiled down the steel
fell through the chair
dropped the left eye &
drove the storm home
drove the storm home.

Kirkuk

For an instant
as he boards the C-17

Red remembers his mother's
first cousin home from the war

counting for hours
on his fingers and toes

and drooling from the curled trap
of his mouth as he sat indian-style

on the floor of their trailer's small kitchen.
In the blink of a minute Red's own

body will hurtle from twelve hundred feet
through the dark loam of night,

a momentary killer

navigating between broken fields
and the parchment sky.

Strange Fruit

We refuse to see that we will not see,
and that keeps us safely from guilt.

Ask the station-man, the utility man, the man
in the cell block. Ask the master of the Humvee,
but he won't recognize either
this need that defines your disorder:
the blight of the first world
that rips flesh from the third.

So drink up your martini
and suck dry the fruit,
slip the noose around the necks of the natives
and strip the bark clean—

thatch hut torched and the naked cheek turned;
reap and then reap and then reap and then burn.

April Snow

3.
Lush, dropping
white from the sky like a blessing
over raised naked beds,
the unraked leaves revealed
from the fall. These
storm warnings have lasted
for more than a week now
under ungiving skies until this—
this engorgement, this deluge.

2.
In the other world
rivers flow into themselves
like oxbows conjoined.
Where they converge there's a silence
and my thoughts are given
to wander over the unbroken shoals
that lie peaceful beneath,
a kind of *pax mortalis* for the mind.

1.
But here the snow falls
from a sky that's besieged.
The shape of our fear moves toward
the unknown and fearing that,
we seek to name names. A contrail
becomes a sea snake, a child becomes
god. The bombs that we drop
attempt to define this enigma:
Fat Man, Little Boy.
And the people we kill.

Dignity

You can see it in their eyes,
much as you can see any thing
if you look hard enough.

It's not hard for the villagers
who wear the expressions of their ancestors,
long since resolved to the
tenets of progress. Honest in the face of deceit,
through the duplicity
of all that you bring them—lotions and
granola, designer shampoos,
mirrors from the First World laid on a pillow.
They understand the semantics
of charity; they will grant you your pity.

But don't pity the villagers.
They are blind to your wealth,
your laissez-faire waste.
Because when the scythe blade swings
the machete descends,
you will run from the riverbed parched—

Cortez, reviled, blood sticks to your fingers.

Cut Piece

Yoko Ono cut naked
in the whelp of Japan,
then decades later
on the banks of the Seine.

So much love endowed
by the revealing of ego:
birthmark, palm scars,
obsidian gaze trained
out the open box window.

Too much love?
Never too much.

Safe Passage

In the clipped half-light
between the highway and glass
I met death yet again.

Yet again
as though I'd always met death
right here on this bus, always this night
with the still moon on the wane over Wellstone
and other historical ghosts only recently past,
all of them moving through us
on this slow roll to Washington
to meet democracy by morning.

*

I'll say this: I haven't missed this rain—
or I've forgotten now
what it could possibly mean:
weak-kneed, slack-jawed,
my neck a burnt piece of sausage. The
slap slap of wipers against the windshield.

It's just that now upon waking,
it feels different—this dream, this death—
feels better than I ever remembered it.
It feels like this night, surrounded by friends
whose names I don't know but whose
cores I imagine my own core
to be: without malice, laid open clean.
The way humans can be
when they're able to choose.

But there was this also—
lust
a going-in and a coming-out
but bloodless, a kind of thruway
Like this road to the Potomac; further
among the children of the ghost-dance
who pass in their red-yellow bus.

Further among the fear in the suburbs
and yet that fear fades because
we make it fade. We are all, after all,
in death as in life, waltzing the rain,
we are dancing with ghosts.

I'll say this: I would die for my country.
I would die for my country if it would live up to me.

Pledge

Not this for which I stand:
this madness,
this malevolence of arms,
this single finger thrust into the air.

Brought to the cliff's edge
we are taught the water's demise,
but dare not to bear witness
to the foam's bold coupling
with the broken black shore.
Always this lesson, this
same
  old
    lesson,
        and yet
I continue to want
more from two souls
united by flesh—
a pact between mortals
still scared of the dark.

It is this for which I stand,
for which I continue to dream:
to be mortal and believe,
to learn laughter between screams.

Memorial Day

Hanging clothes, Memorial Day.
Three hours since the procession
threaded through the depot
and now the summer screams
from the Little League field behind Blue Market.
Billy plays the line behind third base,
and I can hear his own clear voice sound out from the rest:
HeyyyybatterbatterbatterSwwing!
His hands are fast like mine,
and when he throws to first
his wristbands flash like battle flags.

When I finish pinning his clothes,
I'll stand at the sidelines with other parents,
some cooler-fed, some quiet. Black flies
will be biting, but no mosquitoes—not yet.

At the parade this morning I couldn't answer
Billy's questions about combat. Instead I lied
about the beauty of medals and marching in formation,
about differences between places but not between people.
How to explain that tools become weapons, that fear becomes hate?
How to explain that I don't know why, that I will die not knowing.

Billy showers after the game, then calls his mother.
Propped on the couch with a magazine open
I listen for a voice I can't understand
even though I still try.
Every few minutes I flip through a page
to let Billy believe that I'm reading.

Hermit Thrush

"The essence of the superrich is absence.
They're always demonstrating they can afford
to be someplace else." —John Updike

I always enjoy the dream
where the small birds defend us,
lightning troves of hermit
thrush in a line above us
as we climb Lincoln Peak.
The dream begins

where our feet leave off,
off the dim granite edge and
into the dark. The cat tracks we follow
lead to heliodor mansions now gouged
into the hills, ringed by rock walls
and stone-pillared gates. Nobody's home
so we go inside

gilt-edged mirrors line the great halls
verdantique floors and glass chandeliers,
claw-footed tubs adorn the boudoir—

and yet the place is still empty,
still empty and still.

I'm hungry you tell me,
and when I glance in the mirror I can see
that we've both sprouted talons, have grown ourselves wings;
when you turn toward the window the moon glints off your beak.

They'll never miss these, you tell me,
as you row a dozen swiss chocolates under your wing.

But we've got to do something, I'm yelling,
the river is ruined, the mountain's been mined!—

Relax, you laugh, drooling Cristal
through your black-sequined feathers.
Don't worry the ruins. And remember:
we'll be here long after they're gone.

Jamie Gage is a Vermonter, father and husband, poet and writer who has won fellowships to the Vermont Studio Center and Vermont Council on the Arts. His work has been published in dozens of periodicals and literary journals including *Main Street Rag, Inkwell, Out of Line, Mountain Gazette, Powhatan Review,* and others.

A freelance writer and web services professional, Jamie is interested in grassroots organizations that focus on the arts and education, community advocacy, technology, and lasting, systemic change. He lives in central Vermont where he enjoys writing and music, winter sports, and spending time with his family.